P9-CED-595

Dear Parent:

Congratulations! Your child is taking the first steps on an exciting journey. The destination? Independent reading!

STEP INTO READING® will help your child get there. The program offers books at five levels that accompany children from their first attempts at reading to reading success. Each step includes fun stories, fiction and nonfiction, and colorful art. There are also Step into Reading Sticker Books, Step into Reading Math Readers, and Step into Reading Phonics Readers— a complete literacy program with something to interest every child.

Learning to Read, Step by Step!

Ready to Read Preschool–Kindergarten
• big type and easy words • rhyme and rhythm • picture clues
For children who know the alphabet and are eager to begin reading.

Reading with Help Preschool–Grade 1
• basic vocabulary • short sentences • simple stories
For children who recognize familiar words and sound out new words with help.

Reading on Your Own Grades 1–3
• engaging characters • easy-to-follow plots • popular topics
For children who are ready to read on their own.

Reading Paragraphs Grades 2–3
• challenging vocabulary • short paragraphs • exciting stories
For newly independent readers who read simple sentences with confidence.

Ready for Chapters Grades 2–4
• chapters • longer paragraphs • full-color art
For children who want to take the plunge into chapter books but still like colorful pictures.

STEP INTO READING® is designed to give every child a successful reading experience. The grade levels are only guides. Children can progress through the steps at their own speed, developing confidence in their reading, no matter what their grade.

Remember, a lifetime love of reading starts with a single step!

For Luke Easter, from a fan
—J.O'C.

For Roberto Clemente
—J.B.

Photo credits: pp. 9, 38 (top left), AP/Wide World Photos; cover, Hulton Archive/Getty Images; pp. 1, 26, 29, 32, 38 (bottom right), 47, National Baseball Library, Cooperstown, N.Y.; pp. 14–15, 38 (bottom left and top right), courtesy of National Baseball Library; p. 41, UPI/Bettmann Newsphotos.

Text copyright © 1989 by Jim O'Connor. Illustrations copyright © 1989 by Jim Butcher. All rights reserved under International and Pan-American Copyright Conventions. Published in the United States by Random House Children's Books, a division of Random House, Inc., New York, and simultaneously in Canada by Random House of Canada Limited, Toronto.

www.stepintoreading.com

Educators and librarians, for a variety of teaching tools, visit us at www.randomhouse.com/teachers

Library of Congress Cataloging-in-Publication Data
O'Connor, Jim.
Jackie Robinson and the story of all-black baseball / by Jim O'Connor ; illustrated by Jim Butcher.
    p.   cm. — (Step into reading. A step 5 book)
SUMMARY: Presents a biography of the first black baseball player to play in the major leagues when he joined the Brooklyn Dodgers in 1947. Also traces the history of all-black baseball teams.
ISBN 0-394-82456-3 (trade) — ISBN 0-394-92456-8 (lib. bdg.)
1. Robinson, Jackie, 1919–1972—Juvenile literature.
2. Baseball players—United States—Biography—Juvenile literature.
3. African American baseball players—Biography—Juvenile literature.
4. Baseball—United States—History—Juvenile literature.
5. Negro leagues—United States—History—Juvenile literature. [1. Robinson, Jackie, 1919–1972.
2. Baseball players. 3. African Americans—Biography.] I. Butcher, Jim, ill. II. Title.
III. Series: Step into reading. Step 5 book.
GV865.R6027 2003 796.357'092—dc21 2002153806

Printed in the United States of America   31 30 29 28 27

STEP INTO READING, RANDOM HOUSE, and the Random House colophon are registered trademarks of Random House, Inc.

JACKIE ROBINSON

AND THE STORY OF
ALL-BLACK BASEBALL

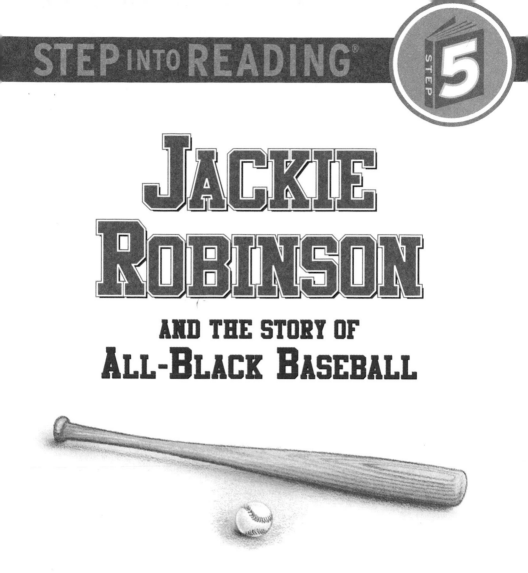

by Jim O'Connor

illustrated by Jim Butcher

Random House 🏠 New York

ALEXANDRIA LIBRARY
ALEXANDRIA, VA 22304

1

Jackie Makes History

April 15, 1947

It is opening day at Ebbets Field, the home of the Brooklyn Dodgers. Today they are playing the Boston Braves. The crowd is excited. The crowd is always excited on opening day. But this day is special for another reason.

All along the third-base line fans peer across the bright green diamond. They try to see the new player that the whole country has been talking about.

He is over in the Dodgers' dugout. He sits by himself. He looks nervous, and his teammates leave him alone.

Soon the announcer begins to call out the Dodgers' names. One by one the players run out onto the field. The stands erupt with a deafening roar. Finally the new player's name is called. Someone pats him on the back. Then he jogs to first base with a funny pigeon-toed stride that soon will be famous everywhere.

Who is this player? And why is this day so special?

He is Jackie Robinson. He's twenty-seven years old. And he's just become the first black man to play major-league baseball in the twentieth century.

Today about a quarter of all major-league ballplayers are black. But in 1947 the world is a very different place. Many hotels will not give rooms to black people. Many restaurants will not serve food to black people. In the South there are separate schools for white children and black children. Even

drinking fountains have signs. They say "For whites only."

For more than fifty years major-league baseball has been for whites only too. But not anymore. Not with Jackie Robinson in the Dodger lineup.

Black fans have their hopes riding on Jackie. They know it is not easy being the first man to cross the "color line" in baseball.

During the season Jackie is booed by people in the stands. They call him awful names. They tell him to go back to the cotton fields, where he belongs.

On the field it isn't any better. Pitchers throw bean balls—balls aimed right at Jackie's head. Runners try to spike him with the sharp cleats on their shoes.

At home he gets hate mail. There are letters that threaten to kill him, beat up his wife, and kidnap their baby son.

The pressure gets to Jackie. After only a

few games he falls into a batting slump. He makes an out twenty times before getting a hit.

But Jackie doesn't quit. It is hard to take the insults without fighting back. It is hard to be "the first." But he knows one thing. If other black players are to get a chance in the big leagues, he has to keep quiet and keep playing.

Jackie pulls out of his slump and starts showing what he's got. By the end of the season he is hitting .296. He leads the Dodgers in runs scored and stolen bases. He has belted twelve home runs—the most any Dodger has hit this season.

With every hit, with every stolen base, with every run scored, Jackie wins more fans. Wherever the Dodgers play, the stands are packed with people who want to see Jackie. There is even a train just for fans going to some Dodgers-Reds games in Cincinnati. It is called the Jackie Robinson Special.

By the middle of the season other teams start signing up black players too. It is the beginning of the end for whites-only baseball.

But it's the beginning of the end for all-black baseball too.

For nearly seventy years there have been professional all-black baseball teams. They have never been allowed in the major leagues. But they have had their own leagues. The Negro leagues. Up to now they have given thousands of black players their only chance to play pro baseball. But now all that is changing. As the big stars of black baseball sign up with major-league teams, the Negro leagues grow weaker. Fans stop coming to the games.

Fourteen years after Jackie Robinson's first game with the Dodgers, the Negro leagues are wiped out. A forgotten chapter in baseball history.

2

Barnstorming

Pro baseball was born soon after the Civil War. For the first time men started playing baseball for a living. Not just for fun. In those early days there were a few black players on different teams. They were good— just as good as their white teammates. But they always got cut or traded. All because of the color of their skin.

Bud Fowler was the first black to play pro baseball. People who saw him said he was a great second baseman. But no club would keep him. One season he was on five different teams.

The story goes that it was Bud Fowler who invented shin guards. Before a game he would tape pieces of wood around his lower legs. It was the only way he could protect himself from all the players who tried to spike him.

Bud Fowler once said, "The color of my skin is against me." And he was right.

By 1899 black players were completely shut out of pro baseball. No team owners would hire them. But that didn't stop black players—they started up teams of their own.

The first all-black team was called the Cuban Giants. It was started by a group of waiters at a hotel in Babylon, New York. Nobody on the team was really Cuban. But during games they pretended to speak Spanish. They did this because they thought white fans would come to see Cubans play. Even Cubans with very dark skin. But they were afraid no white fans would ever watch ordinary black Americans play baseball.

Right away the Cuban Giants were a hit with black fans. At last they had a team they could root for. Soon more black teams sprang up. Because the Cuban Giants were so popular, other teams used Giants in their name too. There were the Leland Giants. The Columbia Giants. There was even a team called the Cuban X Giants!

Nearly all the black teams were from big cities. Places like New York, Chicago, Philadelphia, Pittsburgh. Sometimes the black teams played games against each other. But

they did not belong to a real league that set up games for them. Not like the big all-white teams. Most of the time the black clubs just traveled on a team bus from town to town, looking for a game wherever they could find one. This was called barnstorming.

Barnstorming brought really great baseball to out-of-the-way places. Back then there was no TV. The only way to see a baseball game was to *be* at a baseball game. And America in those days was really baseball crazy. It was the number one sport. So when a good black team arrived in a small town, it was like a holiday. Factories might shut down early. Schools sometimes closed for half a day. The whole town—blacks and whites—would turn out to see the black team play ball!

Barnstorming meant spending weeks on the road. It was a hard way of life. Especially in the South. Often no hotels or restaurants let in blacks. So the teams had to eat and sleep right on their bus. Sometimes in warm weather they slept by the side of the road. Sometimes they even slept on the bleachers at the ball fields.

Barnstorming meant playing in all kinds of places. One day a team might play in a real ballpark with stands and a scoreboard. The next day they might play in a school-yard. Or even a cow pasture! That didn't bother the black teams. They were pros. And they would play wherever there were paying fans.

Most of all barnstorming meant playing lots and lots of baseball. To make enough money, teams squeezed in two and even three games a day. Sunset was the only thing that stopped them. After all, they couldn't play in the dark. And once good electric lights came into use, darkness didn't stop them either! Black teams were the first, in fact, to play night games. They just brought big lights along with them.

Then, after the last inning was over, down came the lights and the tired players would climb back on their bus. It was time to head for the next town and the next game.

Barnstorming was too tough a life for some players. After a season or two they quit baseball.

But most players stayed on the road for as long as they could. They made pretty good money at a time when black people often had trouble getting any kind of job. Maybe they weren't in the major leagues. But they did have lots of fans—black *and* white fans. And when they put on their uniforms and ran out onto the field, they were doing what they loved best. Playing baseball.

3

"Smart Baseball"

Nobody ever did more for black baseball than a man named Rube Foster. He wanted black baseball to be just as well run, just as well respected, as the major leagues. And he spent nearly his whole life trying to make it that way.

Rube started out in 1907 as a pitcher for a team in Chicago called the Leland Giants. He was a good baseball player. But he turned out to be an even better baseball manager.

In 1911 Rube started up a new team called the Chicago American Giants. And what a team it was. Rube got all the best black players of the day. But he knew it took more than raw talent to make a powerhouse of a club.

Most black teams did not get a lot of coaching. There was no time for that on the road. Players just joined a team and went out and played. But Rube drilled his team in what he called "smart baseball."

Black baseball was a lot different from white baseball. White baseball came to depend on home-run hitters like Babe Ruth to win games. But black baseball did not.

On black teams pitchers were allowed to throw all kinds of tricky pitches. They could throw a spitball. They could throw a "shine ball." That meant the ball had a little Vaseline rubbed on it. Pitchers could also nick or scratch the ball. That made it jump and dip on the way to the plate.

This kind of pitching made it harder to hit a homer. So Rube made his players work on getting a piece of the ball. That meant getting a base hit. In this kind of game bunting was very important. So Rube sometimes put a hat inside the baselines. He made his players learn to bunt right into it!

Rube wanted players who were fast runners, players who stole lots of bases. This made the games exciting. And it brought the American Giants lots of victories.

Rube was from Texas and called everybody "darlin'." But any player who didn't listen to Rube was in BIG trouble. During games Rube always sat smoking a pipe. He used his pipe to give signals to the players. If he puffed it one way, that meant the batter should bunt. If he puffed it another way, that meant the man at first should steal second.

And that's just what the players would do if they wanted to stay with the American Giants.

Rube wanted a real baseball home for his team, even though hardly any black teams had stadiums of their own. When black teams played in a big city, they had to rent a ballpark from a major-league team. They had to pay a lot of money, and they could only play there while the major-league team was out of town. Sometimes the black teams weren't even allowed to use the showers or the locker rooms. That wasn't good enough for Rube. He saw to it that a stadium was built for his team. It could seat 9,000 people.

All of Rube's hard work paid off. The American Giants were so popular that sometimes they drew bigger crowds than the Cubs or the White Sox—Chicago's two major-league teams—when all three teams were playing on the same day.

Rube hoped to have a team that was so good, the whole team would be asked to join the major leagues. It would be the first black major-league club. That didn't happen. But in 1920 Rube did start a league for the best black teams of the day. It was called the Negro National League. It set up games between teams. And it set down rules for players.

But then in 1926 Rube Foster got very sick. He had to retire from baseball. He died in 1930. And two years later his league died too.

Did this mean the end of black baseball? Far from it. The 1930s and 1940s became the golden age of black baseball. And the superstar of this golden age was a pitcher with an arm of iron. A man named Satchel Paige.

4

The Great Satchel

No pitcher in the history of baseball can match Satchel Paige. Usually pitchers wear out faster than other players. Their arms go from so much throwing. But Satchel was never your usual pitcher. His career stretched over forty years and thousands of games. He was around sixty when he finally stopped pitching!

LeRoy Paige was born in Alabama sometime in the early 1900s. No one, including Satchel, was ever sure of his exact birthday. He got his nickname when he was just a little boy. He used to earn extra money carrying people's satchels at the train station.

In 1924 Satchel pitched his first pro game for the Mobile Tigers. It was the first of about two hundred and fifty teams Satchel played for.

Satchel was tall and thin. Almost skinny. But when he reared back and threw the ball, he was throwing *fire*. He had one of the most feared fastballs of all time.

Satchel had different names for his fast-ball. Sometimes he called it his "bee ball." Or "trouble ball." Or "jump ball." Or "Long Tom." Whatever its name, the batter knew one thing. He had to be really sharp to hit it!

Satchel joined the Pittsburgh Crawfords in 1932. The team was started by a black man named Gus Greenlee, who was involved in gambling. He wanted to build the best team in the history of black baseball. And he did. Five members of the Crawfords are now in the Baseball Hall of Fame.

Catcher Josh Gibson was almost as famous as Satchel. Josh was called the black Babe Ruth because he hit so many home runs. One season he hit eighty-nine—that was twenty-nine more than the Babe's record. But this record didn't count because Josh was not on a major-league team.

Josh Gibson's short, smooth swing rocketed the ball over fences everywhere. His most famous homer was in Yankee Stadium.

Another black team had rented the stadium for a game with the Crawfords. When it was his turn at bat, Josh hit the ball so hard and so far, it flew over the left-field stands. It went right out of the park. No other player—not Dave Winfield, not Mickey Mantle, not even Babe Ruth—has ever done that.

Judy Johnson was another famous teammate of Satchel's. He played third base for the Crawfords. Like all great players at the "hot corner," Judy was quick as a cat and had a rifle arm.

Oscar Charleston usually played first base for the Crawfords. But he was such a great all-around athlete that he could play any position. And sometimes that is just what he did. He'd play all nine positions in a single game!

Cool Papa Bell played outfield for the Crawfords. The fans loved him because he was such a bold base runner. He turned singles into doubles and doubles into triples or

Judy Johnson (above), Oscar Charleston (above right), and Cool Papa Bell played together for the Pittsburgh Crawfords.

homers. Nobody could run as fast as Cool Papa. Satchel often roomed with Cool Papa Bell. He once said that Cool Papa could flip off a light switch and be in bed before the room was dark! That might be one of Satchel's tall tales. But anyone who saw Cool Papa knew he was the fastest runner around.

Not only did Gus Greenlee put together a great team, he brought back the Negro National League. That was the league Rube Foster had started. In 1937 a second league was formed. The Negro American League. There were lots of good teams around, but the Crawfords were tops. And wherever they played, the star attraction was always Satchel.

Satchel had no change-up or curve ball. But he won game after game with his blazing fastball and his amazing confidence. Sometimes Satchel was so sure he would win, he would tell the batter exactly what kind of pitch he was going to throw. And still he'd strike the batter out. Other times he would order his outfield off the field!

In barnstorming games Satchel pitched against some of the greatest white major-league pitchers of the day. And he beat them. Satchel earned more money than most white players in the major leagues.

Here is Satchel Paige with Dizzy Dean, the best major-league pitcher of his time. Dizzy played against Satchel in barnstorming games and called him the greatest pitcher ever.

Still, he was a black man. And he had to live with prejudice. He would not play in any city where he and his teammates could not get a decent hotel and a decent meal.

He played on all-black baseball teams for almost forty years. That was some record.

Like Jackie Robinson, Satchel finally did get to the major leagues. And he set a record there, too. It's a record that will never be broken. Satchel became the oldest rookie in baseball history when the Cleveland Indians took him on in 1948.

The Cleveland Indians were in a tight race for the American League pennant that year. They needed another good pitcher. Satchel filled the bill. Satchel was either thirty-nine, forty-two, or forty-eight at the time. He had a 6–1 season, and the Cleveland Indians did go on to clinch the pennant *and* win the World Series.

Satchel only lasted two seasons with the Indians. But he kept on pitching until 1965.

Lots of people, including Satchel himself, thought Satchel should have been the very first black player on a major-league team. It didn't work out that way. But Satchel never had anything except great things to say about the man who was the first. Jackie Robinson.

5

Crossing the Color Line

In 1945, World War II was over. It was a war for freedom. It was a war in which thousands of black soldiers had given their lives. "If a black man is good enough to die for his country," many people were saying, "he's good enough to play baseball."

But was there a white baseball man with the guts to be the first to sign a black player? And was there a black player with the guts to be the first?

The answer to both questions was yes!

Branch Rickey was the president and

general manager of the Brooklyn Dodgers. He had been managing baseball teams nearly all his life. More than anything, he wanted the Dodgers to win the World Series.

The Dodgers were an old team. They needed new, young players. Branch Rickey knew there were some really good young black players in the Negro leagues. He was willing to sign some if it meant his team could win the Series.

Branch Rickey wanted to bring a black into major-league baseball for another reason too.

Many years ago he had been the coach of a college baseball team. The team had only one black player.

On a trip to Indiana the black player was told he couldn't stay in the hotel with the rest of the team. Branch Rickey finally got the hotel to let the man room with him. Later, when Branch went to the room, he found the man sitting on his bed. He was staring at his hands.

"Black skin!" he cried out. "Oh, if only it was white."

Branch Rickey saw how cruel it was to judge a man by the color of his skin. It was something he never forgot. But he knew he had to find a very special black player to cross the color line. And he wanted to keep the search quiet. So Branch Rickey announced that he was starting a new black team. The Brooklyn Brown Dodgers. This was just a trick. It let Branch send out his baseball scouts. They could look openly for the best players on the black teams. Not even the scouts knew the real reason why Branch was interested in the black players.

One of the scouts soon singled out a young shortstop on the Kansas City Monarchs.

Jackie Robinson is your man, the scout told Branch Rickey.

Jackie Robinson was born in 1919 and grew up in Pasadena, California. His family was poor. But Jackie was smart, and Jackie was great at sports. In college he was a star on the football team. And the track team. And the basketball team. And the baseball team.

In World War II, Jackie became an officer of an all-black unit in the army. He was one of the very first black officers.

He was a man who always stood up for his rights. When he was in the army, Jackie lived in Texas. At that time blacks had to sit in the back of city buses, in the worst seats. But on army buses blacks got to sit wherever they wanted. One time Jackie got on an army bus. The driver told him to get in back. But Jackie refused to do it. The bus driver had him arrested! Jackie went on trial, and he was found not guilty.

Jackie could have done what the bus driver said. But he was not that kind of person. He was willing to go through a lot for what was right. This was important to Branch Rickey.

Branch Rickey asked Jackie Robinson to come to Brooklyn to meet him. Jackie was not sure why Branch Rickey wanted to see him so badly. But he soon found out!

Branch told him flat out. He wanted Jackie Robinson for his team. The Brooklyn Dodgers. Not the Brooklyn Brown Dodgers.

Then Branch gave Jackie a taste of what he was going to hear from fans and players on other teams. For three hours he called Jackie every bad name. He described all kinds of mean situations. Then he told Jackie, "You cannot respond to any of this."

Jackie asked, "Do you want a ballplayer who's afraid to fight back?"

"I want a ballplayer with the guts *not* to fight back," Branch answered. "If you fight or answer the insults, you will lose. And so will all the other black players who are waiting to play. You must promise me that you will hold your temper and your tongue."

Jackie Robinson made that promise. On October 25, 1945, he signed a contract with Branch Rickey. It was big news on sports pages all across the country. In black newspapers it made front-page headlines.

Many people thought Branch Rickey made the wrong choice. Even players in the Negro leagues. Jackie Robinson was a rookie, people pointed out. He had played only one year with the Monarchs. Yes, he was a good hitter and a daring base runner. But out in the field he wasn't that great.

Branch knew all this. But he had a plan. Jackie would start out with the Montreal Royals. This was a farm team for the Dodgers. It was a place where young players like Jackie could get training for the major leagues.

The 1946 season was a good one for the Montreal Royals. And a good one for Jackie, too. He played well, and the fans liked him.

The next year Jackie was ready for the Dodgers. But right away there was trouble.

During spring training some Dodgers said they would sign a letter. The letter demanded that Jackie get off the team.

The manager of the team found out about the letter. He called all the players together. He told them that Jackie was staying. Anyone who didn't want to play with him could go to another team. That was the end of the letter. But there was more trouble.

Right at the start of the season, two

teams said they would not play against the Dodgers. They would go on strike. The teams were the Philadelphia Phillies and the St. Louis Cardinals. But the president of the league was tough. If the two teams wouldn't play, he promised to throw them out of the league for the rest of the season. That was the end of the strike. But that was still not the end of the trouble.

A few weeks later the Phillies arrived at Ebbets Field for their first game with the Dodgers. From the moment the game started, the Phillies called Jackie every name in the book.

Jackie could do nothing. He could say nothing. He'd made a promise to Branch Rickey. The other Dodgers knew this. And they felt bad for Jackie.

The next day the Dodgers told the Phillies and their manager to leave Jackie alone. Even the Dodgers who wanted to keep Jackie off the team stuck up for him now.

The games went on. There were more hard times ahead for Jackie. But he knew one thing. He really and truly was one of the Dodgers.

For ten seasons Jackie Robinson played second base for the Brooklyn Dodgers. He played in six World Series. He was voted Most Valuable Player in 1949. His lifetime batting average was .311. In 1962 he was elected to the Baseball Hall of Fame. It was another first. No black man had ever received this honor before.

But for millions of fans Jackie Robinson meant so much more than awards and averages. He was not just a hero for black people. He was a hero for the whole country.

6

A Place of Honor

Every year about 300,000 people visit the Baseball Hall of Fame in Cooperstown, New York. Fans read the names on the plaques. They read about the records these men set. For a baseball player there is no greater honor.

Until the 1970s no Negro league players were in the Hall of Fame. Hardly any were eligible, because they had never played on major-league teams. But whose fault was that, anyway?

When Ted Williams, the great Red Sox slugger, was voted into the Hall of Fame in

1966, he said, "I hope that someday Satchel Paige and Josh Gibson will be voted into the Hall of Fame as symbols of the great Negro players who are not here only because they weren't given a chance."

Ted Williams's wish came true.

In the late 1960s the rules were changed so that the superstars of the Negro leagues could get the honor they deserved. Satchel Paige was the first. He was elected to the Hall of Fame in 1971. Josh Gibson came next, along with Buck Leonard, in 1972. So far, out of more than 200 Hall of Famers, eleven are players who made their name in the Negro leagues.

At last, at long last, they are where they belong.